In the Galley with Graham
Recipes used on Tenacious

Illustrated by Keith Bacon
Edited and Project Managed by Pauline Appleby

Cover picture copyright © Max. www.tallshipstock.com
Poems written by Ann Goodhall
Back cover photo © Gemma Telford

Published in Great Britain by
Interface Event Management & PR Ltd
Upper Street, Defford, Worcs WR8 9AB

Copyright © Graham Samways & Pauline Appleby 2006
Illustrations and design © Keith Bacon
Printed by Goodmanbaylis

First published 2006

ISBN 0-9553392-0-0 978-0-9553392-0-2

In the Galley with Graham

Recipes used on Tenacious

Illustrated by Keith Bacon

Profits from the sale of this publication will be donated to the Jubilee Sailing Trust
www.jst.org.uk

Graham would like to acknowledge two people in particular who inspired his interest in cookery from an early age. Firstly his mother, Gill Samways, who by her own standards of cooking set him on the path in the first instance. Secondly Jamie Oliver, whose enthusiasm and casual approach to cooking has awakened the potential cook or chef in many a young man!

As well as those of Jamie Oliver, other recipe books that take pride of place on Graham's bookshelf include the Australian Woman's Weekly series of cookbooks and the Milk Marketing Board's Dairy Book of Home Cookery, which in his opinion contains without doubt the most consistent and accurate recipes available.

Foreword

Thank you for supporting the Jubilee Sailing Trust....

I am incredibly proud to have been involved with the Jubilee Sailing Trust since 1996.

The unique and special design of the ships, the LORD NELSON and TENACIOUS, ensure mixed ability teams can work side by side on all sailing tasks as well as sharing the more relaxed times. I have complete admiration at the way the JST provides for such striking teamwork between disabled and able-bodied people. They change lives for the better and their work is to be commended.

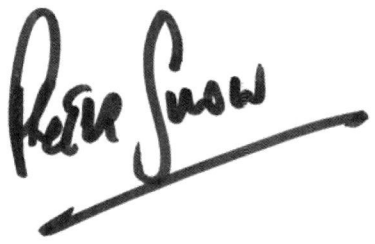

Vice Patron – Jubilee Sailing Trust

Contents

Introduction

It was never going to be easy. For a start, the man with the recipes is always at sea, the quantities he cooks for would make most people jump overboard, and the methodolcgy comprised of words like "spaff", "splosh", "wack" and "shove". However, ever seeking adventure I was not to be deterred, and the idea of a cook book started to become a reality. A chance meeting with renowned marine artist and fellow JST stalwart Keith Bacon in Scarborough during the Tall Ships' Race 2005 really set wheels in motion, especially when I discovered he also had graphic design skills!

Having decided on the recipes to include, my first task was to reduce the quantities and re-write the methodology so that readers wouldn't need an English/Graham dictionary at their side. However, having played around with the recipes it was vital to check they still work so a team of trusty volunteers, many being fellow crew from recent voyages, were issued with several recipes each to try out. We have included many of their comments, tips and serving suggestions throughout.

Some of the ingredients were originally listed in weight form, and some by 'cup'. My first instinct was to put them all into a standard format, but in fact it's so easy to cook by cup (especially if you are reading this on a boat!) so I have left them as they were. Please note that a cup is a standard English teacup, not a mug!

As a vegetarian myself I'm glad that most of the meat dishes have veggie alternatives so there is something for everyone, and I would make a personal plea for you to use free range eggs. I would also ask that you consider using free range and organic meat.

On behalf of Graham, Keith and myself, there are many people to thank in the production of this book. All of the testers, without whom I'm not sure what we would be inflicting on the unsuspecting public! Max, for allowing us to use one of his wonderful photographs of Tenacious for the front cover. Annie ("The Dame") Goodhall for letting us include some of her beautiful poems. And all of the permanent crew and voyage crew we have sailed with over the years, who have given us inspiration, laughter and friendship.

Pauline Appleby
Summer 06

About the Jubilee Sailing Trust

The JST is a UK based charity (registered charity number 277810) that aims to promote the integration of able-bodied and physically disabled people through adventure tall ship sailing holidays. The JST welcomes people of all ages and from all over the world onto its two specially designed tall ships the Lord Nelson and Tenacious.

Each ship is able to take a voyage crew of 40, who sail alongside the professional crew of 10. The voyage crew is divided into 20 able-bodied voyagers and 20 disabled voyagers, including up to eight wheelchair users. To date the JST has taken well over 26,800 people to sea; over 10,500 of them have been disabled and nearly 4,000 of those have been wheelchair users. The ships have been designed with many special features, ensuring that everyone on board is able to take a full and active part in the running of the vessel.

Tenacious was built and constructed by the Jubilee Sailing Trust at their own Jubilee Yard. She was built by a team of professional shipwrights and volunteers of mixed ability bringing the JST ethos of integration ashore. She is the largest wooden tall ship of her kind to be built in the UK in the last 100 years and her Maiden Voyage was 1 September 2000. Since then she has taken over 4,800 people to sea, of these over 1,800 have been physically disabled. Since commencing voyages in 2000 Tenacious has sailed over 100,000 miles.

In order to fulfil the aims of the JST and to be able to run and maintain the two wonderful ships, the JST relies on charitable donations. If you would like to support the aims of the JST, or sponsor an individual to sail please visit www.jst.org.uk.

"Nothing beats the thrill of sailing a tall ship. Why not come and try it for yourself?"

*Amanda Butcher,
Chief Executive*

DREAM

I dreamt the sea last night
The sweet salt smell
Gull cries and glitter.
Sharp grains of sand,
Opal flecked flakes of flint
The sea frozen in stone, brittle.
I felt the limpets sucking cling
Crabs sideways clicking.
Shells sinking in soft ooze.
Heard wind born wailing,
Storm birds seeking shelter
And foam hushing on the beaches.
Saw water eddying around rocks
Pushing out the seaweed
Pulling in bleached driftwood
Swirling memories.
When I dreamt the sea last night.

Ann Goodhall

Smoko
(Known ashore as coffee break!)

Shortbread

250g plain flour
125g rice flour or semolina

250g butter
125g caster sugar

pinch salt

Combine the two flours and add a pinch of salt.

Stir in the sugar.

Cut the butter into small pieces and rub into the flour/sugar mixture.

The resulting mixture should resemble a not-too moist dough and leave the sides of the bowl clean.

Use to fill an 8-inch (20cm) sandwich tin.

Press firmly down into the tin and prick all over with a fork.

Bake at 180°c (350ºf or Gas 4) for 15-20 minutes until golden brown.

Remove from the oven and sprinkle lightly with extra sugar.

Tip: Do not open oven during cooking!

Serve on its own, covered with chocolate or with a fresh fruit salad.

Cook's Assistants aren't what they used to be!

Nutmeg Cake

1 cup self-raising flour
1 cup plain flour
1 teaspoon ground nutmeg
125g butter

1½ cups soft brown sugar
1 teaspoon bicarbonate of soda
¾ cup milk
1 egg, lightly beaten

½ cup chopped walnuts or pecan nuts

Grease an 8-inch (20cm) sandwich or cake tin.

Sift the flours and nutmeg into a bowl.

Cut the butter into small pieces and rub into the flour.

Stir in the sugar.

Press 1½ cups of the mixture into the cake tin.

Stir the bicarbonate of soda into the remainder of the mixture.

Then stir in the milk, egg and chopped nuts.

When well mixed, pour onto the dry mixture already in the cake tin.

Bake at 180°c (350°f or Gas 4) for 30 mins.

Sultana Cake

3 cups sultanas
250g softened butter
¾ cup caster sugar
5 eggs

2½ cups plain flour
¼ cup self-raising flour
¼ cup brandy
1 teaspoon vanilla essence

Grated zest of ½ lemon
Grated zest of ½ orange

Soak the sultanas for 2 hours in the brandy. Drain the brandy and keep for use later. Spread the sultanas over a piece of kitchen roll, cover and leave overnight. (This ensures that when the sultanas are added to the mixture they don't make the cake too soggy and they don't sink!)

Beat together the butter and sugar.

Stir in the eggs, one at a time, then stir in the flour and sultanas.

Stir in any remaining brandy, the lemon and orange zest and the vanilla essence.

Pour the mixture into a greased 8-inch (20cm) cake tin.

Bake at 160°c (325°f or Gas 3) for 1¾ hours.

Gingerbread

250g plain flour
2 level teaspoons ground ginger
2 level teaspoons cinnamon
225g butter
225g sugar

125g golden syrup
125g black treacle
$\frac{1}{2}$ pint warmed milk, together with
2 level teaspoons bicarbonate of
soda

2 eggs, beaten
6 balls of stem ginger, chopped

Combine the flour, ground ginger and cinnamon in a bowl.

Gently melt the butter, sugar, syrup and treacle in a heavy based saucepan or in a microwave.

Add the chopped ginger to the butter mixture.

Combine the melted butter mixture with flour mixture in a bowl or food processor.

Add the beaten eggs, one at a time.

Add the bicarbonate of soda to the milk and stir into the mixture.
The mixture will be very wet!

As quickly as possible, pour into two greased and lined 2lb baking tins and place in the oven.

Bake at 180°c (350°f or Gas 4) for 35 mins.

Once the loaves have started to cool, remove from tins and peel off the lining paper. Leave to cool on a wire rack.

"Makes a large, very chocolatey and quite dry cake. Very filling, and scrummy. Perfect with crème fraîche or ice-cream and fruit. Popular with my sailing club members!'
"Useful for using up left-over porridge."

Chocolate Porridge Cake
(handed down from Peter Moore, ex-cook on SV Lord Nelson)

1 cup porridge oats
1 cup cold water
Pinch salt
2 cups cocoa

2$\frac{1}{2}$ cups soft brown sugar
2 cups self-raising flour
250g butter, melted
1 teaspoon bicarbonate of soda

4 large eggs
4 cups water

Combine the oats, water and salt over a low heat as if making porridge.

Melt the butter in a separate pan (or bowl in a microwave).

Combine the butter with the oat mixture in a large mixing bowl.

Stir in the cocoa, flour, bicarbonate of soda, eggs, sugar and water.

Pour the mixture into a greased 10-inch (25cm) cake tin.

Bake at 160°c (325°f or Gas 3) for 40-45 minutes.

First Time Aloft

Chewy Brownies

100g butter
100g plain chocolate
300g caster sugar

2 teaspoons vanilla extract
2 large eggs
125g plain flour

2 tablespoons cocoa powder

Melt the butter and chocolate together in either a heavy based pan or a heat-proof bowl over a pan of boiling water.

Mix together the sugar and vanilla extract.

Remove the chocolate mixture from the heat and stir in the sugar/vanilla extract mixture.

Add the eggs, one at a time.

In a separate bowl combine the flour and cocoa powder. Fold this flour mixture into the original mixture.

The mixture should be quite stiff. Transfer into a greased 8-inch (20cm) square cake tin.

Bake at 160ºc (325ºf or Gas 3) for 40 mins.

Note: Brownies should be squidgy when removed from oven – be careful not to overbake. They will be easier to cut into squares if first placed in the fridge for an hour to chill.

Makes 16 Brownies.

Rocky Road (Captain Barbara's favourite!)

200g dark chocolate (or half white and half dark chocolate)
Handful of mixed chopped nuts

½ cup glacé cherries
½ cup marshmallows (omit for veggie option)
½ cup digestive biscuit pieces - optional

Melt the chocolate in a heatproof bowl over boiling water.

Stir in the nuts, cherries, biscuits (if using) and marshmallows.

Pour the mixture into a lined baking tin.

Chill in the fridge until firm.

Eat, savour, enjoy!

Oi! Who's been at the Rocky Road again?

Almond Slice

For the base:
250g plain flour
125g butter
75ml cold water
Pinch salt

For the filling:
150g ground almonds
2 teaspoons almond essence
115g butter, softened
75g caster sugar

2 eggs, beaten
Blackcurrant jam to spread
Sliced almonds to decorate

Cut the butter into cubes and rub into the flour. Add salt.

Add water to make a pastry mix.

Turn out onto a floured board and knead until smooth.

Roll out and line an 8-inch (20 cm) baking tin.

Put to one side.

Combine the almonds, almond essence, butter, sugar and eggs, and stir until well mixed and smooth.

Spread the jam onto the pastry base.

Pour the almond mixture over the jam.

Decorate with the sliced almonds.

Bake at 160°c (325°f or Gas 3) for 30 minutes until golden brown.

Mince Pies with Butterwhirl Topping

For the mince pies:
100g plain flour
50g margarine
pinch salt
1 tablespoon cold water

1 jar pre-prepared or homemade
mincemeat

For the butterwhirl topping:
175g butter, softened

50g icing sugar, sifted
$\frac{1}{2}$ teaspoon vanilla essence
175g plain flour
Clotted cream or double cream,
whipped until stiff, to serve

With cold hands, rub the margarine into the flour until the mixture resembles fine breadcrumbs.

Add the cold water, until a firm dough is produced.

Turn out on a floured board and using a pastry cutter, cut circles to line the individual muffin tins of a greased muffin tray.

Add a tablespoon of mincemeat to the centre of each one.

Put to one side and prepare the butterwhirl topping:

Cream together the butter, sugar and vanilla until light and fluffy.

Using a large spoon, fold in the flour.

Place the mixture into a piping bag and pipe around the top of each mince pie, ensuring the edges are sealed, but leaving a gap in the top.

Cook at 180°c (350°f or Gas 4) until the pies are golden brown.

Pipe double cream, whipped, in the centre of each to serve.

Coconut Pyramids

2 large eggs
225g desiccated coconut

150g caster sugar
6 glacé cherries

LOOKOUT

There's a thingy over there!

Beat the eggs.

Stir in the coconut and sugar.

Leave the mixture to stand for half an hour.

With wet hands, mould large 'dollops' into pyramids and place onto a greased and lined baking sheet.

Decorate with half a cherry on top of the pyramids.

Bake at 180°c (350°f or Gas 4) for 25 mins.

Tip: ensure hands are wet to mould and allow to cool before removing from tray.

Banana Bread

3 bananas, crushed
1 cup sugar
3 tablespoons butter

2 large eggs
2 handfuls of nuts
$\frac{1}{4}$ teaspoon baking powder

1 teaspoon bicarbonate of soda
2 cups plain flour

Combine all the ingredients together in a large bowl or food processor.

Pour the mixture into a greased 2lb bread tin.

Bake at 220°c (425°f or Gas 7) for 45 mins.

And that's it!

Chocolate Chip Cookies

90g butter
1 teaspoon vanilla essence
1 cup caster sugar
1 cup demerara sugar

1 egg, beaten
$\frac{1}{2}$ cup self-raising flour
$\frac{3}{4}$ cup plain flour
$\frac{3}{4}$ cup chocolate pieces

$\frac{1}{2}$ cup chopped pecan nuts
1 tablespoon milk

Beat together the butter, vanilla essence and sugars until pale, light and fluffy.

Add the egg and stir in the flours.

Fold in the chocolate pieces, pecans and milk.

Chill the mixture for half an hour.

Drop spoonfuls of the mixture onto a greased and lined baking tray, leaving space around each of them to spread during cooking.

Cook at 180°c (350°f or Gas 4) for 10 minutes until golden.

Cool and lift to wire racks (if you've not already eaten them!)

Makes approx 24.

Light bites/
Lunches

Fajitas

2 onions, shredded
2 peppers, thinly sliced
250g chopped cooked chicken or
Quorn pieces

6 wraps
Pre-prepared Cajun dressing, or
1 teaspoon cracked pepper
1 teaspoon paprika

1 teaspoon tumeric
1/2 teaspoon chilli powder
1 teaspoon garlic powder

Place chopped onions, peppers and garlic in a wok or heavy based frying pan. Sauté until softened.

Season the chicken (or quorn) with the cracked pepper, paprika, tumeric and chilli, or use Cajun spice.

Toss all ingredients in the wok or pan.

Serve with wraps and potato wedges together with bowls of salsa, guacamole, shredded lettuce, sliced tomatoes, soured cream and grated cheddar.

Warm Duck Salad

For the croutons:
4 thick slices white bread
4 tablespoons vegetable oil

2 little gem lettuces

2 cooked duck breasts,
chopped
2 strips cooked bacon, chopped
¼ ltr sesame oil
¼ ltr soy sauce

¼ ltr red wine vinegar
¼ ltr vegetable oil
1 tablespoon Dijon mustard
¼ ltr caster sugar

Prepare the croutons:

Remove crusts from the bread and cut into small cubes.

Place vegetable oil in a small bowl and add bread cubes, mixing well to ensure all cubes are coated.

Place on a baking sheet and cook for 10 mins in a moderate oven until golden brown.

Leave to cool.

Prepare the sauce:

Boil the red wine vinegar with the sugar until dissolved and leave to cool.

Whisk in the Dijon mustard.

Add the vegetable and sesame oils and soy sauce.

Wash and prepare the lettuce leaves. Toss with the warm chopped duck and bacon.

Pour the prepared sauce over the salad, and sprinkle with croutons.

This recipe isn't part of Graham's repertoire (yet!) but using editorial privilege it finds its way into the book as a guest recipe!

Alison's Pizza

Makes 2 large or 4 small pizzas

2 large or 4 small ready-made Pizza bases
1 jar green pesto or black olive tapenade

200g sun-dried tomatoes in oil, roughly chopped if large
200g tinned artichokes or artichokes in oil, roughly chopped
16 cherry tomatoes
200g crumbly goats cheese

200g red pepper slices (fresh or in oil)
Cracked black pepper
Freshly grated parmesan cheese to serve

Spread the pesto or tapenade thinly over the pizza bases.
Crumble the goats cheese and sprinkle over the pesto.
Divide the pepper, sun-dried tomatoes and artichokes between the pizza bases, piling each ingredient informally onto the bases.
Add the cherry tomatoes and add cracked black pepper to taste.
Bake in a moderate oven (180°c, 350°f or Gas 4) for 10 minutes until the pizza base is golden.

Serve with green salad and sprinkle with finely grated parmesan (and crushed chillies for extra vava-voom!)

Tips: To prevent the topping being too oily, rinse the pepper, sun-dried tomato and artichokes under a cold tap and drain and pat dry on kitchen roll to remove excess oil. When this pizza was cooked for me it was created using a wholemeal deep pizza base and cooked on a barbeque, which was quite wonderful. To prevent charring, brush the bottom of the base lightly with vegetable oil and place directly onto the barbeque grill. Pull down the barbeque cover if there is one, and cook for five minutes until the base is cooked and the topping softened and melting.

Graham's Caesar Salad

2 little gem lettuce
$\frac{1}{2}$ green pepper, thinly sliced
250g cooked chicken pieces (or cooked quorn pieces for veggie alternative)
Croutons (see page 14)

For the dressing:
3fl oz white wine vinegar
$\frac{1}{2}$ tablespoon Dijon mustard
$\frac{1}{2}$ tablespoon Parmesan cheese, grated

$\frac{1}{2}$ anchovy fillet (omit for veggie option)
7fl oz vegetable oil
Salt and pepper to taste
Juice of $\frac{1}{4}$ lemon

Whisk all the dressing ingredients together in a blender.

Wash and prepare salad leaves and the thinly sliced pepper.

Toss the salad with the cooked chicken (or quorn) pieces.

Sprinkle with croutons and the prepared dressing.

Serves 4-6.

Medical Purse Sue's most favourite lunch!

Scotch Eggs

6 eggs
500g sausagemeat
(or sos-mix veggie alternative)

Flour to coat
I egg, beaten

75g seasoned breadcrumbs
Oil for deep fat frying

Two-Six-Heave!

Hard boil the eggs.

Peel and chill.

Prepare the sausagemeat by dividing into 6.

Place the flour, egg and breadcrumbs into three small bowls.

Dip each egg into the f our.

Using your hands form a 1cm coating of sausagemeat around each egg.

Dip back into the flour to coat again.

Dip each egg into the beaten egg.

Roll in the seasoned breadcrumbs.

Reform the eggs and chill before deep frying.

Fry until golden in colour and finish in a hot oven.

Veggie option: Use sos-mix in place of sausagemeat for a popular alternative.

Sausage Plait

1 onion, finely chopped
1 large carrot, grated
454g sausagemeat (or veggie

alternative sos-mix)
375g pack puff pastry
I egg, beaten

1 tablespoon vegetable oil for frying

Place the vegetable oil and chopped onion in a frying pan and sauté until softened. Season with salt and pepper or herbs of choice.

Mix together the cooked onion, grated carrot and sausagemeat.

With floured hands, form into a log shape.

On a floured board roll out the puff pastry into an oblong. Place the sausagemeat in the centre of the pastry.

Either roll into a large sausage roll, or using a sharp knife cut the pastry into strips on either side of the sausagemeat, and use to cover the filling by plaiting.

Brush with the beaten egg.

Place in a hot oven (220ºc, 425ºf or Gas 7) and bake for 20 minutes until the pastry is golden brown.

Serves 6.

Main Courses

Babootee

500g minced lamb
1½ large onions, chopped
Juice and zest of 1 lemon
Juice and zest of 1 orange

250g sultanas
1½ apples, peeled and chopped
¼ pt vegetable stock
1 teaspoon curry powder

1 teaspoon chilli powder
3 large eggs, whisked
¼ cup sliced almonds, to decorate
Salt and pepper

Peel and chop the onions. Place in a large pan with a tablespoon of oil and fry until softened.

Add the minced lamb and cook through (approx 20 minutes), stirring from time to time.

Add the curry, chilli powder and salt and pepper.

Stir in the stock, sultanas and lemon/orange juices and zest.

Add the chopped apples.

Leave to simmer gently for 15-20 mins.

Transfer into a deep oven tray.

Cover with the whisked eggs creating an omelette mixture and sprinkle with the almonds.

Bake in a moderate oven (180°c, 350°f or Gas 4) for approx 15 minutes until the omelette mixture is golden and set.

Serves 4-6.

Fish Pie

450g smoked haddock, chopped
450g salmon, chopped
250g spinach, chopped, sweated and drained

250g cheddar cheese, grated
150ml single cream
525g potatoes, mashed

2 small or 1 large onion(s), finely chopped
Butter for frying

Place butter and chopped onion into a large heavy-based frying pan.

Sauté until softened.

Add the haddock and salmon and stir.

Stir in the spinach, cream and half the cheese and season with salt and pepper.

Stir in mashed potato and transfer to an oven-proof dish.

Sprinkle the remaining cheese on top.

Bake in a moderate oven (180ºc , 350ºf or Gas 4) for 15-20 minutes until golden brown.

Serves 6.

Chicken Breast

stuffed with garlic cream and wrapped in bacon

**3 skinless chicken breasts
200g cream cheese (plain or flavoured)**

**1 clove garlic
1 dessertspoon fresh chopped parsley (or dried)**

**Cracked black pepper
3 slices back bacon**

Finely chop the garlic and add to the cream cheese.

Stir in the parsley and black pepper to taste.

Turn the chicken over onto the smooth side, and make two angled slits with a sharp knife (like an envelope) to open up the breast.

Using a spoon put a third of the cream cheese mixture into each one.

Place chicken breasts into an ovenproof dish, overlapping each slightly.

Using the bacon, wrap each breast and tuck the bacon underneath to seal.

Bake in a moderate oven (180°c, 350°f or Gas 4) for 45 minutes - one hour until the bacon and chicken are cooked thoroughly.

Serves 3.

Storing Ship

Spicy Pasta

75-100g of penne pasta per person, cooked al dente
125g diced smoky bacon
8in spicy Chorizo or Pepperami sausage, chopped to the same size as the bacon pieces.

425g tin tomatoes, chopped
2 tablespoons tomato puree
1 onion, sliced
1 red pepper, sliced
Handful of fresh spinach
1 clove garlic, chopped

2 teaspoons Cajun spice (to taste)
1 teaspoon granulated sugar
Vegetable oil for cooking
1 dessertspoon olive oil

Mess Duty

Prepare the sauce:

Gently fry the onion and garlic in the vegetable oil over a low heat for approx 5-10 minutes until softened.

Add the bacon and spiced sausage pieces and continue to cook slowly for 5 minutes.

Add the pepper, and continue to cook, stirring all the time.

Add the chopped tomatoes, tomato puree, seasoning and sugar, and leave to simmer for 15 minutes.

In a separate pan, place a knob of butter and a dessertspoon of olive oil. Add the roughly chopped spinach and cook slowly for 3 to 4 minutes.

Stir in the well-drained cooked pasta.

Add the spicy tomato sauce.

Serve with grated parmesan, garlic bread and salad.

Veggie alternative: Use mushrooms and tofu or quorn pieces instead of the bacon and sausage.

Serves 3.

Lamb with Rosemary & Stilton Crust

4 lamb chops or
a rack of lamb, to serve four
50g breadcrumbs

Sprig of fresh rosemary, chopped
150g Stilton or other blue cheese
Milk, to mix

Grate the cheese to the rind into a bowl.

Add the breadcrumbs, cracked pepper to taste and chopped rosemary.

Add enough milk to the dry mixture to make it pliable.

Stir to combine the ingredients to produce a dough-like ball.

Place the lamb into an ovenproof dish and using a sharp knife criss-cross the meat.

Place the dough ball onto the lamb, flatten out using fingers or the back of a spoon.

Roast at 180°c (350°F or Gas 4) for 20-25 minutes until the crust is golden brown and the lamb moist and pink in the middle.

To serve, separate the chops maintaining the crust on each one.

Veggie alternative: Use halved and peeled avocados instead of the lamb. Place on a greased baking tray and grill. You could also use thick aubergine slices, baked in the oven as above.

Serves 4.

OFFICE DREAMING
(APRIL 1988)

The seagulls break the grey town skies
With angry wings and harsh sea cries,
And white on white the air seems full
Of ebb and flow of tidal pull,
And I with wings through winters land
Fly far to reach the cold sea strand,
As through the office window wails
The sound of waves and cracking sails

Ann Goodhall

Vegetable Side Dishes

Vegetable Side Dishes

1 red cabbage, sliced
1 cup red wine
1 cup red wine vinegar
Handful of sultanas
1 tablespoon granulated sugar, to taste
Vegetable oil

Red Cabbage

Sauté the sliced red cabbage in vegetable oil until it starts to soften.

Add the equal amounts of red wine vinegar and red wine.

Add the sultanas and sugar to taste.

1 white cabbage, sliced
Butter
Vegetable oil
Caraway seeds

White Cabbage

Sauté the sliced white cabbage in equal amounts of melted butter and vegetable oil until it starts to soften, stirring to prevent it sticking.

Add caraway seeds to taste and cook over a low heat for five minutes to ensure all the flavours infuse.

Vegetables of choice
Salt
Pepper
Mixed herbs
Olive oil

Roasted Vegetables

Chop vegetables of choice into equal sized chunks.

Season with salt, pepper and mixed herbs.

Toss in olive oil.

Roast in a hot oven (220°c, 425° or Gas 7) for 30 minutes.

Twice Baked Potatoes

4 large baking potatoes
100g butter

200g cheddar cheese, grated
1 onion, finely chopped

Salt and pepper to taste

Wash and prick the potatoes and bake in a hot oven for one hour until cooked.

Remove from the oven and cut each potato in half.

Scoop out the flesh of the potato and place in a large bowl.

Add the butter, cheese and onion. Season with salt and pepper and use to re-fill the potato skins.

Place on a baking tray and return to the oven and cook until golden.

Serves 4.

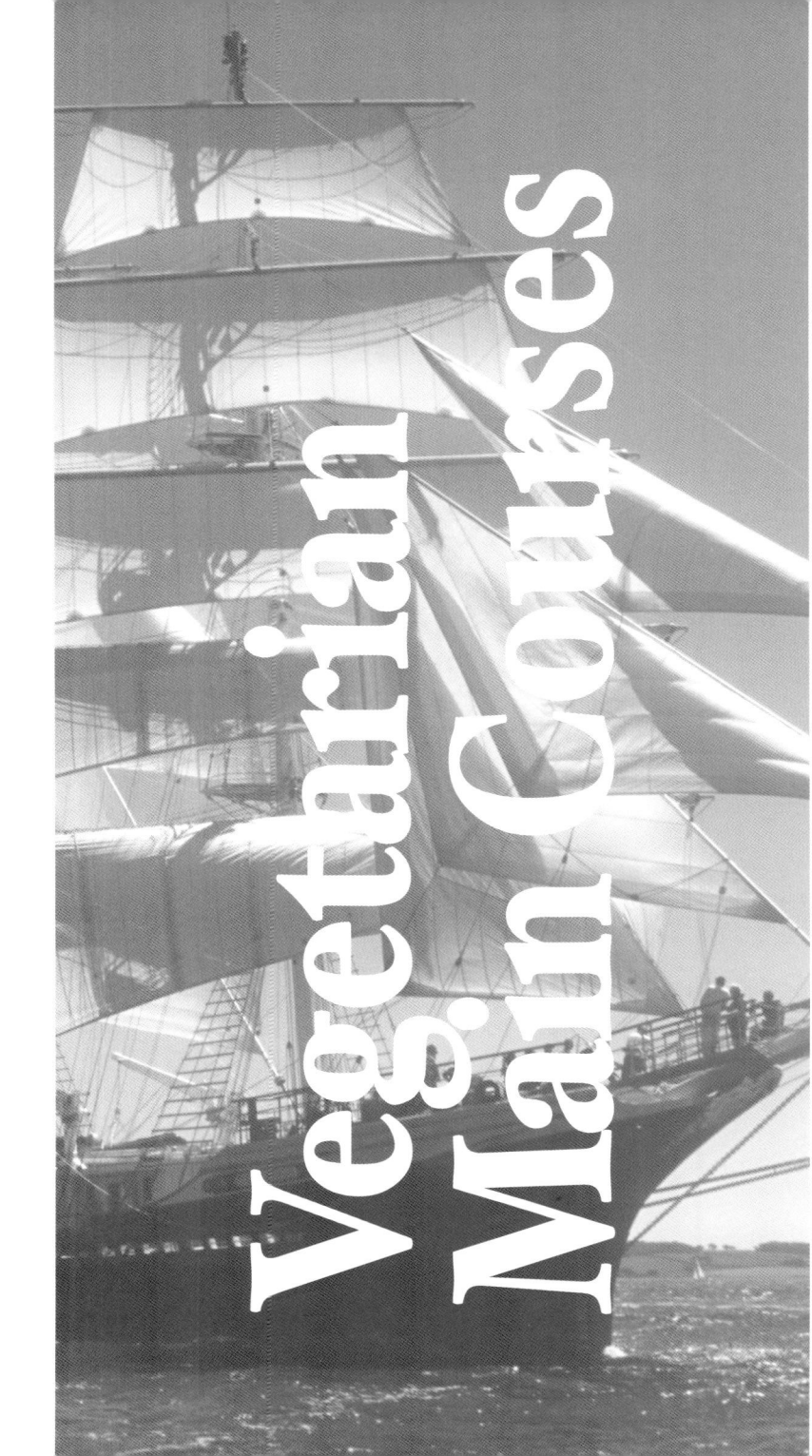

Vegetarian Main Courses

Butternut Squash filled with Cream Cheese

1 butternut squash
250g cream cheese
1 teaspoon finely chopped oregano

Salt and pepper to taste
1 teaspoon garlic, finely chopped
Olive oil

Seasoned breadcrumbs
Grated parmesan

Cut the butternut squash in two.

Scoop out and discard the seeds. Lightly brush the squash with olive oil and place on a baking tray.

Roast in a hot oven (220°c, 425°f or Gas 7) until it starts to soften.

Scoop out the cooked flesh from each half, leaving deep shells.

Chop and combine the removed squash with the cream cheese, seasoning, herbs and garlic.

Push the cheese mix into the squash.

Top with seasoned breadcrumbs and sprinkle with the parmesan cheese.

Return to the oven and bake until golden brown.

Spinach & Goats Cheese Parcel

175g baby spinach, chopped
Pinch nutmeg
Salt and pepper to taste
1 onion, chopped

1 garlic clove, crushed
Butter to fry (approx 30g)
125g log of soft goats cheese
Beaten egg, to brush

4/5 filo pastry sheets or 500g pack puff pastry

Melt the butter. Add the chopped onion and garlic and fry, stirring well, until softened.

Add the chopped spinach, nutmeg, salt and pepper and cook over a gentle heat for 3 minutes, stirring all the time.

Stir in the goats cheese.

If using filo pastry, melt extra butter and use to brush one pastry sheet on a lightly floured board.

Add another filo sheet on top and brush with butter again. Repeat until all the sheets are layered with butter.

If using puff pastry, roll out into a square on a lightly floured board.

Pile the goats cheese and spinach mixture into the centre of the pastry and bring in all four corners to create a parcel.

Using dampened finger tips, seal the edges together.

Brush with beaten egg and bake in a moderate oven (180ºc , 350ºf or Gas 4) for 20 –25 minutes until golden brown.

Serves 4-6.

Oriental Noodles

500g egg noodles
Vegetable oil for frying
1 onion, shredded
1 clove garlic, finely chopped
1 green pepper, thinly sliced

1 red pepper, thinly sliced
400g can baby sweetcorn
250g can water chestnuts
Packet beanspouts
400g can bamboo shoots

Bunch of spring onions, shredded
250g button mushrooms
400g can Hoi Sin sauce or
Sweet and Sour Sauce

(All measurements are approximate and can be increased or reduced according to taste, without affecting the recipe)

Soak the noodles in boiling water for 10 minutes or according to the instructions on the pack. Drain and put to one side.

Heat a tablespoon of oil in a heavy based frying pan or wok.

Add all ingredients and stir fry for 5 minutes until just cooked but still firm.

Add Hoi Sin or Sweet and Sour sauce.

Toss in the noodles.

Warm through in moderate oven (180°c, 350°f or Gas 4) for 5 minutes.

Serves 4.

NIGHTWATCH

The stars dance in the rigging whilst below the
world's asleep
And the moon's a ghost of silver on an ocean wide
and deep
The sails are slapping softly in a cool breeze from
the west
Where the sky is faintly gilded from a sun sunk into rest
The stars dance in the rigging as they only dance at sea
And my heart is dancing with them as the stars just
dance for me.

The stars dance in the rigging each one a point of light
Embroidered on the mystery they call the Cloak of Night
And the cloak is made of darkness as it wraps the ship
and sea
And tangles with the rigging where the stars are
breaking free
To dance upon the yardarms as they only dance at sea
And my heart is dancing with them as the stars just
dance for me.

Ann Goodhall

Scrummy Desserts

Truffle Torte

70g liquid glucose
225g plain chocolate

1 pt double cream, lightly whipped
100g Amaretti or bourbon biscuits, crushed

3 tablespoons dark rum

Crush the biscuits. (Tip - place in a bag and whack with a rolling pin!)

Lightly grease a 10-inch (25cm) baking tin and spread the crushed biscuits evenly around the bottom of the tin.

Place the chocolate, glucose and rum in a heatproof bowl over a pan of boiling water until the chocolate is melted.

Leave to cool for 5 minutes.

Lightly whip the cream until it forms soft peaks and stir half into the chocolate mixture.

Mix well, then pour the resulting mixture into the remainder of the cream.

Pour the mixture onto the biscuit crumb base.

Cover with cling film and chill overnight.

Dust with cocoa powder to serve.

Serves 10.

Lemon Meringue Pie

One 7-inch pre-prepared sweet pastry case, par-baked

For the filling:
1 dessertspoon butter

Rind and juice of 2 lemons, made up to ½ pint with cold water
4 large dessertspoons caster sugar
2 egg yolks

2 heaped dessertspoons cornflour

For the meringue:
Whites of 2 eggs
75g sugar

Place the butter, lemon juice, sugar, cornflour and water into a saucepan.

Bring to the boil and stir continuously while the ingredients melt together. Turn down the heat a little and continue stirring for three minutes until thickened.

Remove from the heat, allow to cool slightly and stir in the egg yolks and lemon rind.

Pour the filling into the pastry case.

In a clean bowl, whisk the egg whites until they form stiff peaks.

Stir in the sugar and whisk again until stiff.

Use the whisked egg white to completely cover the filling, piling it on top of the pie and using the back of the spoon to create peaks.

Bake at 160ºc (300ºf or Gas 2) for 25 minutes until golden brown.

Serves 6 hungry people!

Clafoutis (almond flavour sponge on a soft fruit base)

115g salted butter, melted
115g caster sugar
6 medium eggs

125ml double cream
115g ground almonds
Zest of 1 orange

6 tablespoons soft fruit, ie
raspberries, blackcurrants etc

Grease individual oven-proof ramekin dishes using some extra butter.

Cover the bottom of the dishes with the fruit.

Mix together the melted butter, sugar, eggs, cream, almonds and orange zest.

Divide the mixture between the ramekin dishes covering the fruit.

Cook until set at 1ɛ0°c (395°f or Gas 5) for 25 mins.

Serves 6.

Have you given Graham your suggestions for improving the menus yet?

Pavlova

4 egg whites
pinch salt
250g caster sugar

½ teaspoon vinegar
½ teaspoon vanilla essence
1 teaspoon cornflour

Filling of your choice:
(fruit pie filling, fresh strawberries,
fresh sliced pineapple and cream,
ice cream or crème fraîche)

In a clean, dry bowl whisk the egg whites and half of the sugar together until stiff.

Add the rest of the sugar, together with the salt.

When the mixture is forming stiff peaks, stir in the vinegar and vanilla essence.

Spoon the mixture onto a baking tray lined with greaseproof paper.

Bake in a cool oven (140°c, 275°f or Gas 1) for 2 hours until firm.

Carefully remove from the oven and leave to cool.

Top with cream, crème fraîche or ice-cream and fruit filling of your choice.

Sticky Toffee Pudding

225g chopped dates
290ml tea
110g butter

170g caster sugar
3 eggs
225g self-raising flour

1 teaspoon bicarbonate of soda
1 teaspoon vanilla essence
1 teaspoon strong prepared coffee

Soak the dates in the tea for 20 minutes.

In a separate bowl, cream together the butter and sugar.
Add the eggs, one at a time with a tablespoon of flour.
Then fold in any remaining flour.
Stir in the bicarbonate, vanilla essence, coffee, dates and tea.

Pour the mixture into a greased and lined 8-inch (20cm) deep-sided sandwich tin.

Grease a sheet of greaseproof paper and fold backwards and forwards to make a pleat. Secure over the sandwich tin, enabling the pudding to cook and rise whilst remaining covered.

Cook at 180°c (350°c or Gas 4) for 25 mins.

Butterscotch Sauce

100g butter   **100g demerara sugar**
100g caster sugar   **10fl oz double cream**

Melt the butter and sugars in a heavy based pan.
Stir in the cream and simmer gently for 5 minutes.

Good run ashore?

35

Chocolate Squidgys

150g dark chocolate
125g butter

3 whole eggs + 2 egg yolks
75g caster sugar

75g plain flour

Grease, flour and chill individual oven-proof dishes (ramekins or tin foil dishes).

Melt the chocolate and butter in a heatproof bowl over a pan of boiling water.

In a separate bowl, beat together the eggs and sugar until pale, thick and creamy.

Combine all ingredients and mix until smooth.

Spoon into the chilled dishes and cook at 200°c (400°f, Gas 6) for 6-8 mins.

Serve with cream, crème fraîche or ice-cream.

Serves 6.

Lemon Brûlée

600 ml whipping cream
Zest of 2 lemons

411g jar lemon curd
6 tablespoons demerara sugar

Whisk the cream in a clean dry bowl until just holding peaks.

Stir in the lemon zest.

Add the lemon curd and stir until well blended.

Spoon into heat-proof ramekin dishes and chill for 2 hours.

Cover liberally with demerara sugar and either put under a hot grill or heat with a catering blow torch until the sugar has started to melt and colour.

Leave to cool during which time the sugar topping will harden.

Serves 6

Happy Hour

Chocolate & Baileys Cream Pots

140g dark chocolate
140ml whipping cream

5 tablespoons Baileys or Irish cream liqueur
250g Mascarpone cheese

140g glucose syrup
Chocolate shavings, to decorate

Melt the chocolate in a heatproof bowl over a pan of boiling water.

Add the glucose syrup.

In a separate bowl, whisk the cream until it forms soft peaks.

Stir the Baileys and Mascarpone cheese into the cream.

Combine with the chocolate mix, stirring well to ensure it is thoroughly mixed.

Transfer to individual serving dishes.

Chill until set.

Decorate with chocolate shavings before serving.

Serves 6.

Tiramisu

250g Mascarpone cheese
150ml cold custard
500ml whipping cream
2 tablespoons caster sugar

few drops vanilla essence
Cocoa (for decoration)
50ml Amaretto

200ml strong cold coffee,
sweetened to taste
Packet Amaretti biscuits

Pour the Amaretto into the coffee and put to one side.

In a separate bowl, mix the sugar, whipped cream, Mascarpone cheese, custard and vanilla essence until firm and forming peaks.

Dip the Amaretti biscuits into the coffee mixture and use half the biscuits to line the bottom of a dish (individual or large).

Sprinkle the biscuit base with cocoa powder, then pour on half of the cream/cheese mixture.

Add another layer of biscuits, cocoa powder and cream mixture, until all the mixture is used.

Dust the top with cocoa powder just before serving.

Enjoy!

Serves 8-10.

Cheesecake

400g pack cream cheese
200ml whipping cream
1 teaspoon vanilla essence
Zest and juice of 1 lemon

1 tablespoon caster sugar
1 teaspoon vanilla essence
200g digestive biscuits
1 tablespoon runny honey

50g melted butter
Topping of choice,
e.g. satsumas, black cherries etc

Crush the biscuits or grind in a food processor to crumbs.

Mix together the honey, butter and biscuits until well mixed.

Push into the base of a lightly greased 8-inch (20cm)dish.

Put in the fridge to chill.

Combine the cream cheese, whipping cream, vanilla essence, and lemon zest and juice. Mix until firm.

Pour over the biscuit base and smooth top.

Chill in the fridge.

Decorate with your topping of choice.

(If you prefer a deeper cheesecake, double the cream cheese mixture)

Banoffee Pie

200g digestive biscuits
1 tablespoon runny honey
50g melted butter

4 medium or 2 large bananas,
sliced and sprinkled lightly with
lemon juice

1 can condensed milk
Grated chocolate, cocoa and
double cream to decorate

Put the _unopened_ tin of condensed milk in a deep pan of boiling water for $2\frac{1}{2}$ hours.

DO NOT ALLOW TO BOIL DRY OTHERWISE IT WILL EXPLODE AND MAKE A BIG MESS!!!!

Crush the biscuits or grind in a food processor.

Mix together the honey, butter and biscuit crumbs.

Push into the base of a lightly greased 8-inch (20cm) dish.

Place in the fridge to chill.

After $2\frac{1}{2}$ hours boiling time:

Spread half the sliced banana over the biscuit base.

Remove the condensed milk from the pan and open, _taking great care_ as you do so.

Pour directly onto the banana-topped biscuit mix.

Top with the cream (lightly whipped), remaining banana and grated chocolate.

Dust with cocoa to serve.

Serves 6.

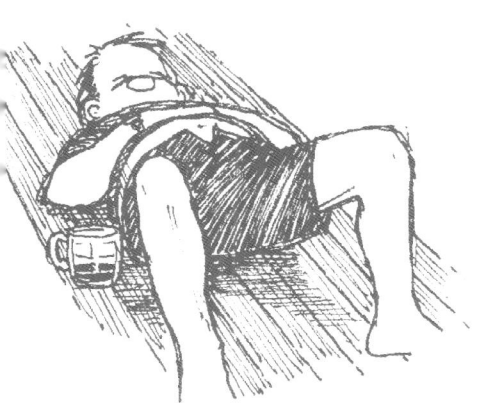

Too much Banoffee!

Jamaican Bread & Butter Pudding

8 slices white bread
150g butter, melted
3 eggs
150ml milk

150ml single cream
2 bananas, sliced
100g chopped dates

3 tablespoons dark rum
1 teaspoon vanilla essence
75g brown sugar

Cut the bread in half diagonally (to produce 16 triangles)

Cover the bottom of an ovenproof dish with a third of the bread, dipped in the melted butter.

Sprinkle with a layer of dates, sliced banana and brown sugar.

Add another third of the butter-soaked bread.

Repeat the layers of dates, banana and brown sugar.

Make sure the final layer is the butter-dipped bread.

In a separate bowl whisk together the milk, eggs, rum, cream and vanilla essence.

Pour half the milk mixture over the bread layers.

Allow the mixture to soak in slowly and repeat.

Press the pudding down and leave to soak for 40 minutes.

Sprinkle with sugar.

Place in oven 180°c (350°f or Gas 4) for 40 mins until golden and set.

Serves 6-8.

About the Cook

Graham Samways has been working for JST since 1996. He is responsible for the production of 1500 meals on-board each 10-day trip, which includes victualling and managing the team of galley staff. Before joining JST, he did a trans Atlantic sail as a trainee on the Tall Ship Astrid and returned to her as a relief cook. Since starting work in the catering industry at the age of 15, he has worked in various hotels and restaurants and at events. Graham was introduced to the Trust by a supporter in Brighton, while working for a dive charter company.

About the Editor

Pauline Appleby is a freelance conference and events organiser with an eclectic background n publishing, marketing, writing and training Guide Dogs for the Blind. Introduced to the Jubilee Sailing Trust in 2000 when using Tenacious as a venue for a corporate reception, she stepped on board and fell in love (with the ship!). Since that life-changing moment she has sailed many times, usually as Cook's Assistant and also as a Watch Leader and has taken up dinghy sailing and scuba diving! Pauline lives in hope that she will one day find a classic yacht in need of a vegetarian cook.

About the Illustrator

After many years in the printing industry, Keith Bacon became a full-time marine artist six years ago, specialising in warships and historical naval actions (and of course Tenacious and Lord Nelson) in both pencil and watercolour. He first sailed with the Jubilee Sailing Trust 20 years ago and has made many trips as Watch Leader since. His work will be familiar to most JST supporters through his Christmas card cartoons and drawings of Tenacious and Lord Nelson.

With special thanks to our team of testers:

Trish and Jonathan Barr

Tom Rogers

Pam Fenna

Emma and Dan Lightfoot

Ruth Brind

Barbara Crompton

Jacqueline Webb

Julya Hobson

Keren Green

Julia Ladds

Shelagh Gartley

Elspeth and John Fisher

Ellen Fenna

Clare and Mark Venning

Michael Bartlett

Derek and Diana Webb

Gwen Bailey

Katherine Stalker

Hilary Dennes

Jean and Norman Day

Notes

Notes